A Short Journey into the Land of the Dead

A Short Journey
into the Land of the Dead

poems

Nick Bonarski

Copyright © 2017 by Nick Bonarski.

Cover image by Kaitlynd J. Malings.

All rights reserved. The use of any part of this publication reproduced or transmitted in any form or by any means whatsoever without the prior written consent of the author, except in the case of reprints in the context of reviews.

ISBN: 978-0-692-97322-6

nick bonarski:
www.scourge-of-the-eigth-sea.tumblr.com

kaitlynd j. malings:
FB: @K.J.Malings
IG: @k.j.malings

First Edition
Published independently by Nick Bonarski

This book is a work of fiction. Names, characters, places, and incidents either are products of the author's imagination or are used fictitiously. Any resemblance to actual events or locales or persons, living or dead, is entirely coincidental.

*Hat's off to Tyler Felty,
this one's for you.*

1

Lecterns. lanterns.
iterations. illuminations. the saplings.
the sopwiths. the waxwings slain.
smoldering.
Sister Mercy. Father Moon.
in the full. in the flesh. flush
bleach. noon. brush. touch. mesh.

so soon. in bloom. ignite,
what's dead.

caverns. patterns.
invitations. inventions. low branches.
glow passions. slow, sweet dew-drop.
drenching.
lemon grass. ginger root.
green teas. greenhorns. grease.
glass. loot. breathe. ease. blessed.

so might.
some night. fly
the nest.

ride the stream. crack the code.
hack the dream.
catch you in the summer.
heat. my cheeks.
owl. fawn. dip pond. croaked frog.

bleed cadmium. hard
cadmium. shyly.
deeply. meet me.

Great Bohdi. Great Banyan
beneath you,
keep me.

A Lullaby for the Damned

O Child, sweet sweet child,
these heavy feet won't do
you're trudging through
the violets
painting the world blue

won't you sit without
them?
Right here next to me?
Dip our toes into the river,
pretend it makes us clean

O Child, sweet sweet child,
don't squeeze your eyes so
tight
I know you're scared but if
you do, your head will hurt
all night

why don't you let it go now?
Let the phantom birds fly
you aren't a nest or
tree-branch
so give them to the sky

O Child, sweet sweet child,
let's go for a stroll
like sideways rain on sunny
days
we'll give the dreamers
pots of gold

How bout' we walk real
slow now? Heel-to-toe light
we'll let the bright
white lilies
be the one's to make
the fields white

Let's go skip some stones kid,
toss the from the other side
like we'd taken the ferry
spit out our coins
after the ride

Maybe your heart's been stolen
Maybe your elbow's badly bruised

But tonight a thief
may keep their hand

and resurfaced hope
may heal you.

Coming along by night in the pale glow
bobbing lanterns in the distance
humming
to the drum and pipe

    hot in the wool I shed my coat
prodding the fire

    they've come upon me, the joyous crowd
the living nomads, the wagoners

    I'm hailed   their dancers approach
in pairs

    do I dare confute the song of
the bone flute and its flexing dreams?

    When sleep calls to me,
and time beckons haste?

    but,

    let us not be so quick
nor waste the flushing moment

    there is always a corner of merriment
carved out the woods, when
coincidence
presents a slender hand

  and the night is young, full as an apple in
Eden to be gained from the extended branch

  the endless infinite turning wheel
carrying knowledge to be passed to those
famished, healing travelers

  as who were they once, but myself?
beside the fire entranced with coal

  be it of the home or the soul
or as shield from cold

  Who knows the good times better than they?

  the exiled, the runaway

  who can teach the common joy better than those
who've suffered and continued on

  who better I ask? they are the teachers,
my gift a student

  and ever the feet to dance.

The world was lit with
candles
    they grew wires inside
        of glass
and so,

the world was lit
with lamps
    but what of the stars?
and first
it was lit by the sun,
    but what of the
        magma core?

Now, it's lit with
fireworks
    now with skyscrapers and
        laser lights
but *what of the stars?*

They are more than myths and
novelties
    and what of the myths?
    Like stars
they'll still be here when
the skyscrapers fall,
    when the fireworks
        have subsided
and the filament's
    burned through

like what we are made of
will still hold
    buried down inside of us

at the center of the world
there is the core
    still filled with the fire of
        burning magma

    but what of the darkness?
      What makes it?

The Doctor

I met a man who made a habit
    of creating light bulbs

it seemed silly to me
    but he was obsessed, even good at it

I named him 'the doctor'
    for the way he builds each bulb
    with precision and patience
    with tongs and steel gauze
    and goggles filled with fire

each new bulb spread open
    on his workbench; a patient
    on a surgery bed

once I watched him cut his hand
    on a fractured piece of glass

"Don't ask," he said, "what the blood'
    is for. The less you know, the more
    the bulb will shine for you."

I told him I'd prefer the room
    a little dim to being blind

"My blood's the only thing
    that gives a bulb its life,
        but at a terrible cost.

If you turn one on
  you'll see me hidden in the shadows

  of each light."

The closer I looked
  the more I realized it was
  true

Now, if you turn on the
  lights

    You'll see me, too.

The postman wears rabbit ears
two years have gone by
and in my youth
dolefully, my friends and I left
a full fresh head
to rot
in the mailbox

it's getting dark
so i captured the fire of my heart
and placed it in an empty bottle
to guide me through

there are many things in the dark
all of them scare me, though i fight them
away

if i cling to you, you will not stay

Take this for yourself

dead reckoning
bludgeoned skull weight
of words

turn it in the dark

shine it through the
sockets&sutures

rockets of dust
coins under alters
candle singed cobwebs

a cavern in the
mountains
bone chimes that hang

dangling red glow
eyes in disguise
with fires alight

on rugs of purple fuzz
with growing succulents
vines on the reddened walls
absorbing the moonlight

"roll it up,
and walk away,
save it for the rain."

say nothing.

something *has*
arisen

like **sleepy**
wheat grass

through a fine
leather vest

underneath a
willow tree

My Sheeta,
like a thief i'd steal you
cut away your ruby hair ties
but do you dare
run with a loner like i?

swords and scimitars,
swiped wine, all of this
to take you to
the lost city on my mind
Sheeta, would you then still
be fine?

if over time
your fires dim, could i
start them in your hands?

or do you dare not trust
a fool as i to bare the light?

suns and warm-blood,
love-crime, come to this

i'll catch you every time
Sheeta, i'll keep you from
the vacuous depths of the
Volucite mine.

In the night
she plays a lyre
and sings all alone

moon down upon her
she gazes up the brittle road

"I left you in Villarie
never to return

"without you sweet Rosemary and the
summer in your eyes,
I left you there with will-o-wisps
in our homeland's tear

"I left you there, Rosemary
by the willow tree,
though you should be here."

"I left you in the hidden place
we found as little ones

"I left you where you held my face
when we would meet at night

"I left you with the flowers we left
on Bill Pickman's grave

"I left you, my dear Rosemary
but I am not
brave

"without you
my Rose "

when the gods ordered
the strings snapped
out of their own guilt

In a Hellish Forest

I watch a hand pulling threads
out of the leaves for
every second that I stay here
is a second of unease

I hear the fowls singing lowly
in the trees
this uncertainty is pairing
with the worst of me

and there is fire dripping
inside of my chest
there is fire growing, burning
all the foliage

I cannot see it but I taste it
on my breath
as I keep along the trail
marked for perfect
death

there's a siren crying thinly
through the air
I feel it tugging me for
every step I'm drawing near

and when I make it I'll tell
everyone to stay clear
or else make love
to all the phantoms that
reside here

like I made love to every phantom
that resides here

The Rakehell looms
in its slow arm guise
in a copse of
gnarling spines
and bramble rose

ramblings under breath chide
and drunk upon the sour-sweets
of plants for the maddening

fickle and sickle
swinging vines rine
the slender branches back
to whip-crack!

The Rakehell steals fire
from the fireflies.

In his sunken
stupor he slinks along
whistling his foul song
throughout the forest old

in the moonlight of forlorn night
searching for his soul.

Run Princess
sweet boy, kind girl
through the reanimated grave-
yard
my darling, mi amigo
        my lovey inner child

        run from the ragged
hands of the undead

run with light legs
wads of burning sage
        in your hands

        smudge all of the
nightmares into half-moon ghouls

prairie kiss the stars
        let them linger in your
skin
        my sweet prince
you little bride
slay the terrors of the night

        or the nightmares will try
to bite, so run princess
but don't forget that
        you're in control

        of this life

A famous crow beckons to a famous vulture
        as refugees flee to a city in the west

    and six-shot death
    unloads fire into the train car;

    everyone inside
    begins to pray

two of us are laying down silent in a bush
        waiting for the doe in the glade to spring

        when the bullet hits with a resonating thud
        a singer leans forward to bury her face

the city's mayor proclaims
    "Get em' outta here! Get em' outta here!"

    while his showgirl feeds him
    grapes from her teet

    the town folk hold a jolly lynching
    in the middle of main street.

the doe kicks in circles 'til its life is done
to feed the one percent of the chosen ones

the vulture leans forward with a warning to the crow:
    "I reckon the distance holds a coming storm"

    the crow recoils, and clacking his beak:
    "I know, I know... and the globe is getting
        damn warm."

Straw Man

I love crows,
used to throw glances
at them

now they sit on my arms

Hark old sparrow
    let me show you to the Pharaoh
    and lands you've never known
    may you know them one by one
    stretching warm soft gold
    across your mind
    sunlight for miles
    and palm trees for your brothers
    along the Nile

my sparrow,
    will you weave into
    our history, imprint your
    supple shape to the glyphs?
    I beckon thee
    beyond thy wildest dreams
    will you not be the one
    to lift our souls
    once our lives flee?

The seasons keep changing
from winter
to spring
to winter
while the phantom of a child
is waiting in the wings

I remember as my friend boarded
the train with her belongings

I woke to her that morning
undressing
while it rained
redressing
brushing split ends from her hair
imprinting beauty on my brain

though I begged for her to stay
she swore she had to leave the city

then whispered as she left
"Please don't worry,
besides, I look
prettier
when I'm on my own."

and the child that she bore
needed a family and a home

now the summer' started snowing
and the fall

blooms white
chrysanthemums
the führer on his throne
rallies troops at the border

and I wonder if her child has turned
to stone:

        her word never comes

but then I saw her in a dream
 pulling weeds
digging ditches
on her knees
as though bewitched she claimed
that she couldn't recall leaving

in the evening we paint the room blue
in the morning tanks roll through

Two crows in my arms
and asleep at my feet
weary yellow stray

Smoke Alarm

maybe it was that
there was an invisible fire

or it could be that you're
running dry on battery

but your false alarms
scare me each
and every time

We could burn ourselves away

    like witches on a bed

      with an opulent and tame

         occultist flame,

just saying.

Stay with me through the winter
I'll tie you up and shiver

at the solidarity between my
heart and my hand
and you might slither

through the bindings

like you do between
my life and my dreams

I feel fine, baby
you swear you do

but I can't tell who's eating who
us both so hungry

I tasted you

bit in like an apple

sunk my teeth deep
until the juice ran
I caught it in my glass

it ever fills and empties
just second-hand ticking
the clock ever fills and empties

those invisibles
ghosts and phantoms
slipping through the corners

periphery, love

the sound of the harpsichord
breaking

Deep blue bullets
loaded in, pointed and aimed

her face my desperate
yesterday, odd

for a killer to bite her lip

she looks enthralled
and I just tremble

breathless
waiting to be blown—

Amoretti

kill me quickly
here between the ribs

see if they crack
and the wound

see if it bleeds
bullshit

Excerpt from the travels of the Nameless Stranger

What we do with death is almost as important as what we do with life, but they'll never tell you that.

How many arrows
does it take to point
to the obvious
great cluster

you lost
and it isn't
coming back

all three of those
arrows broke in your
back, they're stuck
into your gut

you're fucked
that's it
stranger, you're fucked
so what can you do?

Dark dark dark lots of
dark can't see much but, yeah
dark—funny little light

Having detached from his body
he no longer has an "I"
he hovers along instead

the first thing he realizes about death
is that it's really not so different from
life. In fact, he concludes
death is simply a perspective change.
He *would* conclude that, too.

It echoes around the effervescence,
green and more complex than it needs to be

the first thing he observes about death
is that aesthetically it looks different from
life. In fact, he concludes...
death is nearly the inverse of life

to his feet he rises up onto the floor
of the inverse forest. His first words are

not actually words. He just laughs. Death
is just as laughable as life to the dead.
But they don't tell you that either.

With small understanding, his last conclusion
is that the dead need sleep.
So for the duration of one hour
he lays down beside his body
and comfortably stares into the endless
glow.

In this ethereal form, he is warm.
This is the slumber of the dead

awakened he is greeted by his official
narrator, Rod Sterling.

He has no knowledge of me, or my legacy
but graciously it seems, he accepts, and I
not unlike a certain famous cricket
reside in his ear.

Together, we make our way across the
Twilight
of The Deathscape.

He crosses a blue bridge
covered in gold stars

the Deathland is generous
with purple flowers

endless in construction
across the flooded

neon river

the souls jig gaily
contort amorphous

read *Finnegan's Wake*
and walk their hyenas

he waits for the ferryman
caught up in the currents

-5

kite flying

in the city of

night time

bluish-greenish

affluent

Slinking along
beside the prom of the dead

he never knew how much
existed down here

outside the world he
knew and it's strange

how much life there is
in death, almost as if

death wasn't *death* at all

-6

oracle in the soot

capital of the dying

silence

of the sea

In the rain
in the snow
you must know
the voice that keeps you

through the cracks
and the thunder
whispers of death-tide
become a bonafide surfer

in the cold wind
or the whales mouth
start a fire
ride the tempest out

if the dead are at the door
or the thieves in disguise
set traps
invite them to their demise

Writing on the Wall

you can try to hide
demons

but I'm coming for you

with wet kisses and open arms
to embrace you

softly

to suffocate you until

you are
crayola pink and over-sweet

candy hearts
in a bowl on God's kitchen
counter, leftovers from

Valentine's Day

There is a garden down in Hell
that no other has seen or heard of

and the Devil goes there to shake
his chains by loving the
beauty and lightness of the world

if you listen close enough,
you can even hear his song
of freedom

erupt from the back of my skull
where he's been singing
for way too long

but now that the secret is out
he can stop torturing me
with contradictions

and catchy show tunes

85

loose gravel and fire
leading up the road

into the dark antechamber
the red heart of
Hell

passing souls along the way
carting out the old

while angels of surprise
compromise their faces, rushing

off at the sound of
chiming alarm bells

the misplaced rags of slaves
abandoned lay beside

Gardens of Serenity, suspended landscapes
to taunt its occupants or keep alive

the last dregs of hope
as some live, and some die

in the hospitality of the devil
who may cry, and

in the stage production
may care

I flipped a coin down into a pool
surrounded by blue flames

and the water swallowed it
whole

filling a bucket full
I let my eyes close

when a spark of light
from the cavernous sky

grew before me

here the devil's throne
engulfed in fire resides

with glittering rubies encrusted
on the seat

you know I stole one,

where was he going to send me?

Heaven?

89

the devil marched us across the fields
of the piss perfume patches of

whatever-flower and fuck-off fantasias

and eventually we caved

I'll never forget
the broken smile of God

when he took off his mask, proclaiming
his passion for stinky flowers
and obscenities and all the things

he forced into poor Lucifer after rolling
him out of clay

"Ain't that the way, ain't that the way"
we sang amid hosannas of joy & praise

"Ain't that just the way it is, baby"

90

an angel stepped out of line
and raised his head to Heaven
decidedly, under the smoke
and fumes
underneath set backs
and atrocities

and Heaven looked down
straight through Hell
giving us cords of light
bound in seamstitcher's
threads, wool shawl wraps
various codings
and coordinates that
the heart may read through
its cipher

to heal the world from
underneath the vestibule
of that strange kind,

"the neutral angel,
Cher Ami."

gold beams
invisible
dawn
arrives

Songbird in the tree
adrift between the worlds
opening the rift

3

Fifty by fifty
rows to dig
alone without a spade

fifty by fifty
rows haunt
each step along the road

unmarked,
and unknown
engulfed in orange flame

I tried to burn my sorrows
with the mass grave, but

fifty by fifty
follow me
everywhere I go

if you wanted a poem of paranoia
then never stop searching, it's hiding in plain sight.

I see the faces of the killed,
the dead

the murder my own mouth
commits, I still see them
when I close my eyes

I hear their voices in my head
sometimes

I'd like to trade places

but this weight is a killer
in itself

and I died on my own
long, long ago

with each of them

There are two lakes joined
by several small channels

my hands are cold on the oars
paddling through the morning

there is no visible life
no echoing cry
around the curve of the stream
no bird in the leaning
bow of the trees of winter

my breath is steam
sharp and heavy as the vessel
docks ice

I remember smoke
billowing across the water
July sometime

rockets of annuals blooming
overhead, mortar fulls of shells,

what you told me then,

and what I lost crossing back

there's snow above my ankles
seeping between the boot
and the sock

is there more time?
Before the sun starts to rise
over top the trees and wind formed
valley's of snow?

Limping across the lake
I hurry to the spot
to brush away what's fallen

and with the blunt of an ax
breach below

for how could I possibly let it go?
Your challenging doubt
and turning to stone?

And every last piece of you
I've come to know
your son and your life
each word of your tome

as if every seraph in heaven alone
could stay the shaking in my bones

the cracking ice splits wide
in the glow
as the sun starts to show

and lighting the fuse
of this red raw stick

it slips silently
to the bottom of the lake

"The last known place
of your still beating heart,
may it be blown wide
apart!"

the blast could be heard
for miles around, but in
a second did subside

though only the boat
was ever found

no other had survived.

The grave, he dug it
lowered her quietly
—calm
closed his eyes for
days.

Phoenix Down

let me kiss those cuts
as a friend with careful lips

does like a mother for her child
from the entrance to the exit

I'll rest my head
listen for night time
through your ribs, it's
lovely here between
unknown breasts

you stir, black drink
dot out lines on my
chest, hardly scared
of permanence

my breathing flees
in rapturous need
buckling knees
give, slain

I restore light to death,
guide the blind to bed
mop the fever
from your forehead
with eyes closed

ignited nebula
rise, again

daddy got a new pair of shoes

I left town,
bought a razor and some clippers
painted up my face like a
porcelain doll
became a ghost, made my head
clear as a monk's

I burned the hair in a pile
on a wooden floor in Albany
in a ring of advent candles. I watched
the hair curl, the blackened fringes
stain the floor, I cut a phoenix
into my arm and returned from the dead
but my body's still asleep somewhere and
my soul is in a jar I don't keep very far
away from it.

Churning earth below the sky

      yellow teeth rot down to the bone

            Marianne sips an ice cool cerveza

            she likes to be alone

Two decanting vials
bubbling vexed fermentation
red drop, blue drip, green simmering
shining orbicular symmetries
[sip beneath the moon, sit between
the slide and the ground]
wait to touch your mouth to the harmonica
who knows what jazz will swathe
it's listener, what salve will solve
their sister'd silage wrenching
the southward air
with sound

Say nothing.

Something is
spilling

the **ooze**
of centuries

into the
CaUldrON of
DEaTh

all the
witches

are
AghAst

Empty Factory

close your eyes, and beside me walk
we have time here

here where the halls house
no clocks ticking near the ceiling

will you take my hand?

There are loose rocks ahead
and I've fallen before

they get to me, those little
pebbles

wobble and hide underneath
the visceral puddles that poured
in

during the floods,

broken glass too passed through
with water

so mind your step— please?

And this— *this* is what I meant to say
so much sooner than I have

that it would be dark here, that
 you wouldn't see much anyway

but I could walk this path alone blindfolded

now, at least. We're almost there

if you don't mind to just step with me
onto this elevator. It *is* fully functional

although the others are down
and
eve— —sorry,
even the building seems to be
fighting the impend— —*well!*

Can you blame it? So old, so long spent rusting

the shaft threatens its own destruction
violent jolting thing

but— Ahhh... even it sighs to a halt eventually.

While we venture into the depths
in search of the fuse box, my friend

to light again the bulbs in this
weathered factory that emptiness has overtaken

all I want to ask you is
with what dreams will you fill it?

Will you fix it up or leave it?

For as I reduce to ash at your feet,

I leave you the keys.

I lifted mine smokey eyes
aye, thine window spread
ye waved te tell: "Come in!"
red! Call it a day's breath ded!
But, ye named me fog. N' now
pray me, return shall I te sin
swear by me mine smokey spouts
taste if pears n' gin
<hic!>

Up the ladder rungs in the tower
at Entna looking out into the horizon
I dream

against the parapet, the wind
penetrates the schema
of the clouds

not for me, but that I bear witness
who would mind if it inspired
the thought that I could
scatter my doubts
and keep moving toward
that place I seek?

The light gives way behind the trees
once again, but wholly new
I could see it set: a thousand wings
maybe more, flying out

the leaves rustle with applause and
the wind finds rest, but the night sky
breathes

and there is a celebration down below
in the city

down below where
the merry
dancers be

I'm washed ashore

my ship's wrecked
my ribs cracked boards
spilling saltwater
blood and luxuries

I want the sea
to keep them

keep my spice and
cannons, keep them
curled in her waves
and all my dead men

hers to crush
in her depths

I am washed ashore

torn asunder
by blunderbuss
ransacked and waylaid
undead with tales to tell
and bottles to fill
with messages
of desperate hope

and a conch to
whisper secrets into

the way the sea does
her millions
that echo onward
a record of her voice

she and I
in this the same

deadly and
alone
dying and
furious
soothing and
tyrannical

still different
by vast amounts

she so keeps me
tethered here where she
carried me

and holds me in the palms
of her deserted island

Sci-fi & Tea

All of my feelings are coming to
a head

we all know

God's consistently dying

and it all seems so
obvious

I wonder how I didn't see
it before

once I round the bend

just suck the gut in

maybe you'll be there this time
in this version of Heaven
some waste-field plain
between reed grass

someone else's dark marsh

through the eyes look
look —

look up into the dome

repetitions and cycles
not close enough

a tablet, a pill, a tongue
dissolves

a street, a holstered
gun

hugs man, and a place
to rest your head

let it go
beg

subterranean anesthetic
scowl, spirit howl

an "I miss you"

October in a colonial town
pumpkin guts spill, laid on the
ground

the halos of saints
glow, but I lost mine long ago
slipped from the ladder

Salem stays, says to Earth:

"What is this midnight land?
Don't know if I like it,

not sure if I can't."

Popping up Daisies

somewhere down there
I still had enough life in me
to return to you as a few

fresh flowers, and the
warm green grass between
your toes,

enough to feed the wild fawn
her first meal in transit
across this old boneyard

and enough even that
I wandered with her for
two miles, and further on

being that I had enough
in me to continue at once
with her, and behind her

where enough of me
fed a fresh moss and a
patch of morels over time

refined on the forest floor
I found there was still enough
in me to be passed around

in a basket to a family and
within the bodies of restaurant
goers, and a brooding chef

so much of me, that I moved
at once through the man
at my smallest levels

and through him to his wife,
to his sweet laughing angel
where I passed you

and smiled from my stroller,
where my eyes glowed looking
up at you, recognizing

how much of me you've carried
all this time, and I never left
not once, still laying down

beneath the soil & the daisy stems

for you

shh a quiet

the movement
downward

smoothing dirt
all away

from the mound
stretching edges

of the landing
grounds

at an ancient temple
a concert hall
a blooming forest

a living space
full of harmonies
to
fly

around the inside
of your body

driven by a
glass pilot;

whir the
contrails of

fate and destiny
with your
finger

now do the birds sing?

I'll cross the graveyard every night
to see the stones wink names at me

forever in my dreams

I'll let you haunt me
where I can hold you

in this life spent hoping
beyond absurdity
that you'll be born a summer child

and that the daisy's will become sunflowers

whatever they say, the wise
I don't care

you'll always be my girl

The Slide

every time he
opens his eye he sees
excitements
dying, slipping into
an abyss he wishes
wouldn't exist

if only he knew
that he lived on
the slide

and that the fun exists
within the ride

could he learn to
master the thrill
that accompanies
that which he
dreads the most?

Resist the temptation to destroy yourself.
Resist the temptation [**a flock of birds**]elf.
Resist the[**in disarray**]to destroy yourself.
Resist the temptation to destroy yourself.
Resist the temptat[**the sidewalk stretches up the hill, up the stone steps**]oy yourself.
Resist the temptation to destroy yourself.
Resist the temptation to destroy [**flowers leak, limping city morning weeds**]ourself.
Resist the temptation to d[**leaning long in the sun, buildings bend into the street**]elf.
Resist the temptation to destroy yourself.
[**shaded and forgotten**] o destroy yourself.
Resist the temptation to destroy yourself.
Resist the tempt[**its history already lived**]
Resist the temptation to destroy yourself.
Resist [**now you are a child**]troy yourself.
Resist the temptation to [........................]

Easy now— slow now
dear child in gloom

stay now, no no—please!
You musn't move

all of thee, sweet lamb
still of the wood womb

and nest— now hush
and do trust what we say:

pressed myrrh and
silk grass to unthorn
the soul of you,

thistle
and shroom cap of
sweet milky blue

wise wind and berry
bush under the faeries
touch

wings of the sky
holden you...

yes, easy now—slow now
dear child until

you are new

The sky mellowed above the crowd
morphing from blue to burst,
the terse sunset exploding
as would an angry perfumer
judging the flavor
of the flower in the orange puff—
("much too subdued!" and "not remotely close! OH
mandarin is a citrus fruit!")

dazzled,
Merrideth kisses the clock
while I turn the key inside the lock
we both lost track of time;
regained it with pace.

Outside the hotel, marchers in the
street elevate chants that shake
the lobby; diamond earrings drop
like flies, the bellboy sighs as
elegance betrays
the obvious

"they don't understand, but
they are... sort of trying."

leisurely,
Merrideth joins the masquerade
as I step into the parade
we're each hidden ourselves
revealed by our motions

the auditorium crumbles to its knees
trampled by the audience
edging in their seats
just the way the cast wants
"Put the cash
in the bag; hands up in praise—"
the whole act was staged
many months ago,
but the people came
on their own

impressed,
Merrideth pulls the curtains closed
and I take off my clothes
these moments we see
the truth behind the scene

listen to the waves

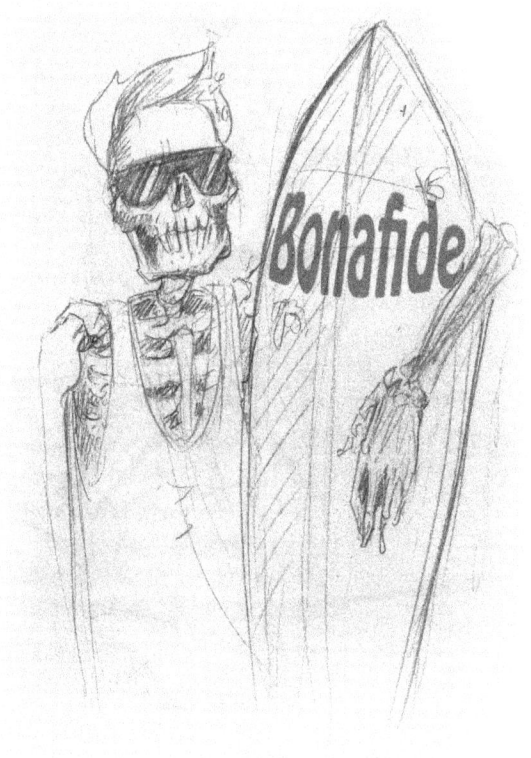

maybe you'll catch one, surfer

Index

1

Lecterns. Lanterns.	3
A Lullaby for the Damned	5
Coming along by night in the pale glow	7
The world was lit with	9
The Doctor	11
The postman wears rabbit ears	13
it's getting dark	14
Take this for yourself	15
Say Nothing//sleepy	16
Sheeta	17
In the night	18
I watch a hand pulling threads	20
The Rakehell	22
Run Princess	23
A famous crow beckons to a famous vulture	24
Straw Man	26
Hark old sparrow	27

1 cont.

The seasons keep changing	28
Two crows in my arms	30
Smoke Alarm	31
We can burn ourselves away	32
Stay with me through the winter	33
I tasted you	34
Deep blue bullets	35
Amoretti	36

Excerpts from the travels of the Nameless Stranger

How many arrows	42
Dark dark dark	43
Having detached from his body	44
He crosses a blue bridge	46
-5	47
Slinking along	48

Nameless Stranger cont.

-6..	49
In the rain.......................................	50
Writing on the wall........................	51
There is a garden down in Hell....	52
85...	53
I flipped a coin down into a pool..	54
89...	55
90...	56
Songbird in the tree........................	57

Part 3

Fifty by fifty.....................................	61
if you wanted a poem of paranoia.......................................	62
I see the faces of the killed............	63
There are two lakes.........................	64
The grave, he dug it........................	67
Phoenix Down.................................	68

3 cont.

Daddy got a new pair of shoes..	69
Churning earth below the sky...	70
Two decanting vials..	71
Say Nothing...	72
Empty Factory..	73
I lifted mine smokey eyes.............................	76
Up the ladder rungs in the tower...	77
I'm washed ashore...	78
Sci-fi & Tea..	80
Popping Up Daisies...	83
For You..	85
I'll cross the graveyard every night..	87
The Slide...	88
Faerie Song..	90
The sky mellowed above the crowd...	91

About the Author

Nick Bonarski lives in Grand Rapids, Mi where he works as an employee for the local hospital. When he isn't working, he's likely scheming, sleeping or writing. If he's not doing any of these, it's because he's spending time with friends and family. Nick is an avid cat lover as well as a sometimes musician.

You can follow his writings here:

@ www.scourge-of-the-eighth-sea.tumblr.com

www.ingramcontent.com/pod-product-compliance
Lightning Source LLC
Chambersburg PA
CBHW032130090426
42743CB00007B/541